Mrs. S. Thorne

For Karen Scawen

Many thanks to the staff and children at
Discovery Montessori Day Nursery, Burnham, Berkshire
and Teeny Tots Nursery, Slough, Berkshire
for their help and advice.

Copyright © 1996 De Agostini Editions Ltd
Illustrations copyright © 1996 Paul Hess

Edited by Anna McQuinn and Ambreen Husain, designed by Sarah Godwin

First published in Great Britain by De Agostini Editions Ltd, Interpark House, 7 Down Street, London W1Y 7DS

A CIP catalogue record for this book is available from the British Library.

ISBN 1-899883-05-3

Printed in Italy by Officine Grafiche De Agostini - Novara
Bound by Legatoria del Verbano S.p.A

Safari
Animals

Illustrated by
PAUL HESS

Zebra

OBSERVING them is difficult,
one quickly loses track
of whether they are black on white
or rather, white on black.

Rhino

"GRIFFY, GRUFFY,"
Goes the rhinoceros.
His horns are pointy
And his feet are thunderous.

Hyena

HYENAS laugh until they choke
But never want to share the joke…

Lion

THE LION has a golden mane
and under it a clever brain.
He lies around and idly roars
and lets the lioness do the chores.

Vulture

HIS EYE is dull, his head is bald,
His neck is growing thinner.
Oh! what a lesson for us all
To only eat at dinner!

Leopard

THE LEOPARD is the sort of cat
You shouldn't keep inside a flat...
He's happiest when running free
Or sleeping in a sun-baked tree.

Wildebeest

THE MAGNIFICENT WILDEBEEST
Wander in herds to follow the rains,
Grazing on the sweet, sweet grass,
That grows on the Serengeti plains.

Elephant

WAY DOWN SOUTH where bananas grow,
A grasshopper stepped on an elephant's toe.
The elephant said, with tears in his eyes,
"Pick on somebody your own size."